My Journey with Jesus

By: Mary Foster

All scripture references in this book are from the New International Version (NIV) Bible.

All the stories within this book are stories about the author and her family.

All inspirational writings were from authors unknown or the author's ideas.

****

Dedication:

Gordon, you are my number one fan and my ever-reliable partner, one of the greatest treasures in my life. God gave you to me, so we could weather life together. Thanks for being my support throughout this endeavor.

Published by: MKF Publishing

2018

A Christmas Story of a Little Girl

In the pre-dawn hours of a Christmas morning, the little girl quietly descended the staircase, being extra careful to avoid stepping on any of the squeaky stairs. She was on a mission and did not want to awaken anyone in the household. When she reached the bottom of the stairs she hesitated, and then gathered courage to cross to her parent's bedroom. She entered the bedroom without knocking.

The little girl quickly moved towards her mom and whispered, "Merry Christmas Mom! I'm sorry I do not have anything to give you for Christmas, all I have is my love." The mom was so touched, she reached up and gave her daughter a hug and said, "That is the best Christmas present I have ever received." The mom encouraged her daughter to tell her dad the same thing. The little girl stood there shaking her head no. After a few encouraging prompts, the little girl reluctantly crossed to her dad's side of the bed. She leaned down and went through the same routine. "Merry Christmas Dad! I'm sorry I don't have anything for you for Christmas, all I have is my love." The dad hugged his daughter and exclaimed "That is the best Christmas present I have ever received." The little girl stood there in the dark staring at her dad, she was screaming in her head: "I don't mean it, I hate you! I hate you!" The little girl was angry and had allowed that anger to turn into hate.

For the rest of his life, and not only at Christmas time, her dad would recall that Christmas story. He would tell everyone about the best present he ever received. There were times when the little girl would hear her dad tell that story and would feel guilty and saddened knowing that his story was filled with untruths.

The little girl loved her mom, she was loving, kind, gentle and all the good things a parent should be. Her dad on the other hand was horribly abusive to her mom and her two older brothers. There were times when the abusiveness was near life-threatening. The stories are varied and better left to the past.

There was an intervention for her dad. He received therapy and the abusive nature ended.

At the age of 11, the little girl accepted Jesus Christ as her Savior. As she grew in her faith her heart changed. God filled her heart with love and forgiveness. The little girl forgave her dad in her heart and learned to love him. She began to appreciate his intelligence, his wit and his dedication to supporting his family. Later in life the little girl began to understand that she had inherited a lot of her dad's traits.

The beautiful part of this story is that Our God is a forgiving God. He opened the little girl's heart and mind to forgiveness. The little girl never revealed to her dad that on that Christmas morning, she had no love for him. The little girl never wanted to crush her dad's heart, so grace entered the picture.

God's plan was to teach that little girl how to forgive and how to love her dad. Her love for her dad was a gradual, trust-inspired, God-given love.

This story is true, the little girl was me. I'm so proud to say that I loved my dad dearly and that I miss him.

Jesus looked at them and said, "With man this is impossible, but with God all things are possible.
Matthew 19:26

No matter the wrong paths we take, no matter how long a journey on a wrong path, God has walked with us and gladly brings us back to the right path.

A Blessed Recovery

Our granddaughter, Addison, was diagnosed with strep throat a few years ago and was given an antibiotic that totally disagreed with her. The medication caused her hands and feet to swell so immensely, she struggled while trying to walk. I was her caregiver during this illness. I found it necessary to carry her wherever she needed to go for the next few days. Her entire body was covered in an under-the-skin blotching. It was a continuing traumatic experience. She was, of course, given another antibiotic. As this began to go into effect, the reaction to the prior medication began to subside. We were praising God that the worst part of this illness was behind us.

After a few days, Addison began to complain her knee hurt, she was beginning to limp. One afternoon after work, her mom picked her up from preschool. The staff related that she had complained about the pain in her knee, so they had carried her around for part of the day.

By the time mom arrived home, Addison was in excruciating pain. A phone call to the doctor revealed an exam at the emergency room would be necessary. Nana and Pop met Mom and Addison at the hospital.

Once in the emergency room, the doctor ordered multiple tests, such x-rays, bloodwork, ultra sound, etc. Every time a nurse or technician entered the room, Addison would panic and start crying. She would ask "What are you going to do to me?" We anxiously awaited test results.

I walked up to Addison and said, "Let's pray." I asked her to repeat after me. She listened to my simple words and repeated them. The prayer was similar to this – "Jesus, I am just a little girl and I'm so scared. Please give me peace. Please help my pain go away." This simple prayer was no more than whispered when a sudden peace enveloped the room. It was evident that God's presence was there. He had answered that little girl's prayer.

A little while later the doctor returned with the test results. He stated she had a septic hip, meaning the strep virus had moved to her hip. The doctor had already been in contact with an orthopedic surgeon. The surgeon agreed to see Addison the next morning, before his regularly scheduled patients.

We were at the surgeon's office before 8:00 am the next morning. The surgeon, being true to his word, saw Addison as the first patient of the day. He agreed with the emergency room doctor's diagnosis, and stated he was willing to perform Addison's surgery that same afternoon. He explained, if left untreated, septic hip could cause her to be permanently crippled. He also stated she would have to use crutches for several days after the surgery.

Addison was taken directly to the hospital and admitted. A successful surgery was performed that afternoon.

The following day I walked into her room, expecting to see her using crutches. She was doing a bit of a hopping technique to maneuver around the room. No crutches for her.

One day while in the hospital room, the chaplain dropped by to see if the family needed his services.

Addison was stressing out again and asked the man, "What are you going to do to me?" He explained he was the chaplain. I then explained to Addison that he was like the children's pastor at church. She looked at the chaplain and said, "Do you know that Jesus died on the cross for our sins?" He replied, "Someone has taught her well!"

So, how many touches did we see from God?

He calmed the room with his presence -

He gave the ER doctor the knowledge for the correct diagnosis -

He gave the orthopedic surgeon the heart to see this little girl in an emergency -

The surgeon performed a successful surgery on the day of her first visit -

Addison did not require crutches -

I have no greater JOY than this; to hear my children walking in the truth.
3 John 1:4 NIV
God is our refuge and strength, an ever-present help in trouble. Therefore we will not fear, though the earth give way and the mountains fall into the heart of the sea.
Psalm 46:1-2 NIV

God Isn't Finished with Me Yet

In 2003 I left work at approximately 4:45 p.m. I climbed into my car and experienced an intense pain in my chest. As I was driving home, I was not too concerned about the pain, I had suffered from acid reflux many times. My concentration was focused on everything I needed to accomplish. The out-of-state company was due to arrive the next day and planned on staying for a few days. Food preparation and housecleaning needed to be finalized. I continued to have chest pains throughout the early evening and night.

I went to work the next day but left at noon. My afternoon was spent making soup and dessert. I was at this point beginning to feel poorly. I would work awhile, then lie down awhile, work awhile and then lie down awhile.

Mid-evening, I called my daughter and explained I was suffering from the worst acid reflux. She came to check on me and stated she was not convinced it was acid reflux. We started towards the hospital, but I insisted that we return home, I was feeling better. She reluctantly took me back home. She kept insisting I go to the emergency room. My response was "My brother is on his way up. He is a fireman/paramedic, he will know if I need medical care."

My brother walked in the door, took my vitals and said, "You are going to the emergency room." I collapsed walking towards the door, he had to carry me to the car.

After the initial examination at the hospital, it was determined that I was in the throes of a heart attack. I was transferred to St. Joseph hospital in South Bend, where an angioplasty was performed. The test showed that I had a 99% blockage. Staff personnel told me over, and over again that I was so very fortunate.

Again in 2016 I ended up in the hospital with breathing difficulties and had another angioplasty. This time I had a 100% blockage. The blood flow through my heart had already begun to reroute itself to make up for the blockages. Both times I needed a stent placed in my heart.

God's protection was covering me. We can come through many trials in our lives and never know why we are spared.

The Lord will sustain him on his sickbed and restore him from his bed of illness.
Psalm 41:3

A Christmas Story

Early one Christmas morning, I walked over to open the living room curtains, to let the early morning light enter the room. When I opened the curtains, my eyes looked down. There on a cold, snowy Christmas morning was an Easter lily in full bloom. My heart melted. This was the day to celebrate the birth of our Lord, Jesus Christ. The Easter lily was a bonus. The lily reminded me that our Savior had died on the cross and was risen on Easter morning.

I was feeling blessed to have Jesus Christ in my heart, I was humbled. I may not have had worldly presents that Christmas morning, but I was reminded of the wonderful gifts God had blessed my life with. I had a loving husband, four beautiful children, shelter and food to fix for this special holiday. I had God's love and mercy and his willingness to die for our sins.

Hallelujah! For the Lord our God, the Almighty reigns!
Revelation 19:6 NIV

Losing a Loved One

After the loss of my husband of 35 years, I was in a near constant state of depression. I cried enough, or so it seemed, to fill both the Pacific and Atlantic oceans. But God did not leave me, no not once.

God knew my heart. I suffered from hysterical meltdowns. During the most difficult times of my struggle, God sent me support. My friend, Gayle, would contact me and talk on the phone, or stop to see me until I was more settled with my emotions. I needed those special touches.

Another meltdown left me feeling overwrought about a document that was needed to finalize a business transaction. I was upset that I could not remember if it was in the file cabinet or the safety deposit box. After struggling with my thoughts, I decided I could at least look through the file cabinet. I lifted the lid of the cabinet and my hand went into the air. My hand automatically reached into the cabinet. When I withdrew my hand, I was holding the necessary document. I had not searched through the cabinet. I felt finding the document was a gift from God.

Good friends are like stairs. You don't always see them, but you know they're always there.

Every good and perfect gift is from above, coming down from the Father of the heavenly lights, who does not change like shifting shadows.
James 1:17 NIV

Crying is a release and a comfort of its own. It allows us to refresh ourselves and release the tension and sorrow that we accumulate.

If God is for us, who can be against us?
Romans 8:31 NIV

The heavens declare the glory of God; the skies proclaim the work of his hands.
Psalm 19:1 NIV

Provisions

When finances were difficult, there was always a solution to resolve the situation, at least temporarily. I can remember a time when we were out of bread, milk, and other necessities. I was wondering where the money would come from to take care of our immediate needs. I went to the mail box to gather the mail. Once inside, I began opening the mail, and saw an official looking envelope from an attorney's office. I opened the letter and began to read. A great, great aunt whom I had never met, had passed away. Because my father was deceased, his portion of the inheritance was to be distributed to me and my six siblings. Enclosed was a check for $23.00 and change. An answer to prayer.

Consider the ravens: they do not sow or reap, they have no storeroom or barn; yet God feeds them. And how much more valuable you are than the birds!
Luke 12:24 NIV

Another time when we were low on funds I walked to the mailbox to discover that after many, many years as a customer with our local utility company, they had decided to refund our initial deposit check.

And my God will supply all your needs according to his glorious riches in glory in Jesus Christ.
Philippians 4:19 NIV

Rejoice in the Lord always. I will say it again: Rejoice! Let your gentleness be evident to all. The Lord is near. Do not be anxious about anything, but in every situation, by prayer and petition, with thanksgiving, present your requests to God. And the peace of God, which transcends all understanding, will guard your hearts and your minds in Christ Jesus.
Philippians 4:4-8

Snowfall

Looking out at a fresh snowfall last night, I pondered varying viewpoints. I would be among the first to send up a dislike about the cold, the slippery roads and sidewalks. However, mixed in with these complaints, there is so much beauty to be found. First off, the cold is too cold for me, yet isn't that first biting breath of cold both refreshing and exhilarating? And the snowflake that falls on your nose, it is as though God is seeking to get your attention and saying, "I am here with you always!"

As you see the individual snowflakes falling how can you not appreciate the beauty? When you consider the fact that each of those hundreds, or thousands of snowflakes are unique, you appreciate the enormity of God's creations.

This could certainly be compared to God's love for us. No matter how unique our personalities, our circumstances in life, our desires, or our struggles, God loves and protects us all on a continuing basis. Our Great Artist has painted a masterpiece when you consider the picturesque beauty of the fresh fallen snow as it clings to the tree lines, fences, etc. it is overwhelming – not unlike God's love for all of us.

As I view the wildlife outside the window on a cold winter day, I am reminded that God's love protects his creatures big and small. None of us are unworthy, God loves us all.

He says to the snow, "Fall on the earth," and to the rain shower, "Be a mighty downpour."
Job 37:6 NIV

As the rain and snow come down from heaven, and do not return to it without watering the earth and making it bud and flourish, so that it yields seed for the sower and bread for the eater, so is my word that goes out from my mouth: It will not return to me empty, but will accomplish what I desire and achieve the purpose for which I sent it.
Isaiah 55:10-11 NIV

Protection

In December 1995, I could have lost my daughter. However, God was protecting her throughout her horrific ordeal. My daughter was preparing to take a bath and discovered the bath water was too hot. She began to walk into the adjoining bedroom to grab a robe.

An intruder was in her bedroom. A struggle with the intruder had her fighting and struggling with him as he stabbed her repeatedly. The struggle continued from the bedroom to the bathroom.

At one time her four-year-old son caught a glimpse of the intruder. He ran into his bedroom and hid.

The struggle continued until my daughter slumped to the floor. The intruder fled but stood outside the back door. When he discovered that my daughter was up and moving, he re-entered the home and a further struggle ensued. When the intruder was forced out the door, the door was immediately locked.

Struggling to survive, my daughter managed to make it to the kitchen to dial 911. She dialed 911, but then handed the phone to her four-year-old son. As her son talked into the phone he cried and repeatedly requested of the 911 caller, "Please, don't let my mommy die!"

An off-duty paramedic had stopped by the 911 center and heard the little boy crying on the phone. The other squads were off on other calls. There was no one except him to make the run. He said, "I'll make the run, send help when you can!" God protected my precious daughter by placing this paramedic at the right place at the right time.

After this incident, I prayed many times over for my daughter's heart and body to heal. Her initial injuries limited her ability to do everyday tasks. She moved in with me and the rest of the family until her wounds could heal. She and her husband and son stayed with us for 9 months. She never returned to her home.

It was ten years after her incident, when she called with excitement in her voice. "Mom, guess what I did, just guess?" I had to admit I had no idea what she might be referring to. She said, "Mom, I took a shower all by myself. No one is home, and I took a shower!" This was a monumental feat. It took her ten years after her incident to be able to take a shower with no one else at home.

I had been watching the movie, "The Purpose Driven Life" when she called. The next line in the movie after she hung up was about forgiveness. I felt as though God had spoken to me in a fresh, new way. I gave her a copy of this book without explaining why I thought she needed to read it.

She continued to hold onto the idea that she could not attend church if she could not forgive the intruder. I believe that God started the wheels of progress and I was anxious to see the first turn of the cog. She finally started attending church again, but It took several more years before she finally found it in her heart to forgive her perpetrator.

The perpetrator was released after spending fifteen years in prison, having received time off for good behavior. When she ran into him in public, she approached him, and told him that she had forgiven him. She described the comfort she received from the forgiveness. She told him she was praying that someday he would be able to receive God's healing and be able to move forward with his life.

I continue to pray for my daughter and grandson. They have fought their battles valiantly, but there are still underlying issues they deal with on a continuing basis.

Therefore, as God's chosen people, holy and dearly loved, clothe yourselves with compassion, kindness, humility, gentleness and patience. Bear with each other and forgive whatever grievances you may have against one another. Forgive as the Lord forgave you. And over all these virtues, put on love, which binds them all together in perfect unity.
Colossians 3:12-14 NIV

How many of us have had sleepless nights? What do you do to counter that sleeplessness? Pray! The next time you have a sleepless night, do not offer only a prayer for help but praise God for His multitude of blessings, His love, His kindness, His Support, and His generosity. He is an AWESOME GOD!

Christ sees our broken hearts, our broken spirits, our mistakes, our wrong choices, but he is a forgiving God, he died for all our sins.

Stand firm then, with the belt of truth buckled around your waist, with the breastplate of righteousness in place, and with your feet fitted with the readiness that comes from the gospel of peace. In addition to all this, take up the shield of faith, with which you can extinguish all the flaming arrows of the evil one. Take the helmet of salvation and the sword of the Spirit, which is the word of God.
Ephesians 6:14-17 NIV

Blessings from God

The man whispered "God, speak to me," and a meadowlark sang. But, the man did not hear. So, the man yelled, "God, speak to me," and thunder rolled across the sky. But, the man did not listen. The man looked around and said, "God, let me see you," and a star shone brightly. But, the man did not notice. The man shouted, "God, show me a miracle!" and a life was born. But, the man did not see. So, the man cried out in despair, "Touch me God and let me know you are here!" Whereupon God reached down and touched the man. But, the man brushed the butterfly away and walked on.

Don't miss out on a "Blessing" because it isn't packaged the way you expect. God is good all the time.
Author Unknown

We are not going to heaven because we are holding onto Jesus, but because Jesus is holding on to us!

Beautiful Seasons

A discussion of the seasons would have most people agreeing that spring is wonderful with the budding of trees, the crocus and tulips starting to pop through the ground, and the grass starting to turn green.

Summer brings on the warmest of the seasons with the possibility of picnicking, swimming, gathering of friends, etc.

Most of us would agree to the esthetics of winter, the absolute beauty of the trees and fence lines covered with a heavy-laden wet snow. We can enjoy the snow before it is covered with footprints or begins to turn to slush.

I would have to agree with the beauty of the other seasons, however, the fall colors are my personal favorite.

No matter which season we choose as our favorite, we need to enjoy the beauty that God has created around this world. The next time you are on a drive somewhere, take the time to enjoy the season that you are in and to thank God for the rich bounty of beauty he has presented to us.

Traveling into Michigan, we were blessed with a beautiful autumnal day. The fall colors had progressed from bright oranges, vivid reds and rich yellows to burnt oranges and deep golden yellows. I loved viewing God's artistry as I rode along. It was wonderful traveling for miles and miles and seeing the beauty stretched before us.

Part of the drive consisted of huge trees on either side of the road with branches hanging over the highway. My mind's eye compared it to a tunnel of love. A "Tunnel of God's Love" that is. It was as though God had placed a tunnel in the middle of the road to remind us that his presence is ever near. We can travel through that tunnel every day of our lives. The leaves had changed to deeper, richer, colors, not unlike the richness we receive in our lives as we follow God through our own "Personal Tunnel of Love."

Traveling on a wet, cloudy day we ended up on a Lake Michigan beach. We were able to obtain some great photographic shots of 4-5-foot waves pounding the dock, along with pictures of the lighthouse during the raging storm. God's beauty was still shining through the storm. It makes one realize that although the weather offers up a raging storm, you have God's love in your heart.

The sky today is very cloudy, there are streams of light running through the clouds which seem to touch the earth. I love that scene. It reminds me that He is there for us always. I received warmth from the scene, it was as though God had sent those beautiful rays down specifically for me.

"O Lord God Almighty, who is like you? You are mighty, O Lord and your faithfulness surrounds you. You rule over the surging sea; when its waves mount up, you still them."
Psalm 89:8-9 NIV

Remember that the next time you admire the wonderful things that God has made, you are one of them.

God gave us 86,400 seconds in a day. How many of those have we used to say thank you?

There is no distance away from God that he will not take you back!

Live your days to the fullest, love generously, speak kind words, and leave the rest to God."
Author Unknown

I can do everything through him who gives me strength.
Philippians 4:13 NIV

Delight yourself in the Lord and he will give you the desires of your heart.
Psalm 37:4 NIV

My Grandmother

I remember my grandmother sitting in the family rocking chair and reading her Bible daily. I remember her having long white hair, that she wore it in a tight bun on the top of her head.

I was one of seven rowdy children. One evening my parents left my grandmother in charge of me and my siblings. After arriving home that evening, I remember my parents asking my grandmother "What is going on? We heard the children screaming from a block away!" My grandmother looked up from reading her Bible and said, "Whatever do you mean, I have not heard a peep out of them all evening." Oh, but to be so engrossed in the Bible that you could block out the screaming of seven rowdy children. That is dedication to the Bible.

I have hidden your word in my heart that I might not sin against you.
Psalm 119:11

Safety

We had been traveling for hours when we came upon a bumper-to-bumper traffic situation. There was severe flooding in the surrounding area and traffic was being diverted.

We traveled further on and came to a Y in the road. We had the right-of-way, but three semis took off at the same time. We were trapped in the triangle of those three semis, however, we made it safely through the near mishap.

It ended up taking 3½ hours longer than usual to work our way through the traffic jam, but we arrived home safely. God's protective hand was on us.

But let all who take refuge in you be glad; let them, ever sing for joy. Spread your protection over them, that those who love your name may rejoice in you. For surely, O Lord you bless the righteous; you surround them with favor as with a shield.
Psalm 5:11 NIV

Praying for Others

The last few years God has opened my heart and mind and given me a voice to speak openly to others. As my faith grows, I have more of a desire to share God's word and to pray with others. In the past, I have struggled to share my faith in public. I felt as though I was not as well-informed about scripture as others. I was worried someone might ask me something and I would not have the right answer.

However, I have discovered that a simple hello, a smile, or a compliment will open your heart and mind to a conversation. When I feel God asking me to share with someone, the words or actions have been automatic.

Sometimes in life we need to take baby steps and tip toe through our situations. The most important thing is taking the first step and being confident you will succeed. God is with you no matter how many steps it takes.

I started a conversation with a woman at a local craft store, while she was looking through the discount bin. I inquired about the project she was working on. She explained that she was excited about spending the afternoon with her grandson and was looking for a simple craft.

I carried on the conversation for a minute or two about crafts and she began to open-up to me. She explained that she had been her husband's caregiver for quite a long time. Due to her age, she had recently placed him in a nursing home as she felt she could no longer care for him at home. She was saddened by this change but had made the decision to do what was best for him.

I had one of my 3-D greeting cards with an inspirational verse with me. I offered it to her and stated perhaps it would cheer her. She was on the verge of tears as she read the card. She said "I will put this beautiful card on my husband's dresser. He will be able to see it every day and it will cheer him."
It was such a little thing from me, but it meant a lot to her. We are not put on this earth to see through one another, but to see one another through.

While at a music concert, I noticed the female usher struggling through a difficult evening. She was seating people all around us. A printing error caused seat numbers to be duplicated. Most people were patient with this woman, however, there were some people that were being less than kind. This dear, sweet woman maintained her composure and kept a smile on her face throughout. I could still see the frustration, but she was handling it with dignity. My heart went out to her.

On a trip for refreshments, I passed this woman. I did not say anything to her but handed her one of my greeting cards with an inspirational saying. I turned and walked away.

Later in the evening, I was again headed to the refreshment stand. I again, passed this same woman. She stopped me and gave me a hug and said, "You have no idea how badly I needed that touch of care and love." Blessings come in small doses and sometimes at odd junctures.

Sometimes your joy is the source of your smiles. But sometimes, your smile can be the source of your Joy.

When I was at a local pharmacy, I noticed an elderly woman at the end of the aisle. As I approached her I said hi, she returned a friendly hi, and smiled. I noticed that she had a lovely smile. We both walked on by. I was going to continue to walk away but was prompted to tell her about her pretty smile. I turned around, went back, and told her how lovely her smile was. She thanked me and responded that my comment brightened her day, she needed that.

She continued our conversation by telling me that she was terribly distressed. A family member had called her earlier in the day and described a serious situation regarding her grandson. This matter could possibly lead him to serving time in jail. She was having a difficult time coping with this news. I told her there was power in prayer and that God had a plan. She thanked me and said I was right.

God thank you for that short conversation with this stranger. I told her I would continue to pray for her and her family. The conversation blessed us both. Sometimes the simplest things can make a big difference.

When my husband was in the hospital for a knee replacement I was given the opportunity to reach out to the staff and other patients. I passed out greeting cards and went into patient's rooms to offer encouragement and pray for those who were receptive.

As you can see, I initiated simple conversations, but God prompted those conversations. These small actions were small deeds, but those small touches were what was needed at every juncture. These incidents were blessings not only to the people involved, but to me as well.

God's heart is the most sensitive and tender of all. No act goes unnoticed, no matter how insignificant or small. I'm not where I need to be but thank God I'm not where I used to be.

Today someone asked me if I knew you. I laughed and said, "HA. That is funny! I adore that woman! She's a blessed, caring, loving, obedient, sweet, beautiful, woman of God. She's reading this message right now. I love her."

For nothing is impossible with God.
Luke 1:17 NIV

If we hold onto the pain of yesterday, we just strengthen it.

If we hold onto the laughter of yesterday, we can let it bloom.

If it doesn't challenge you, it won't change you.

If it doesn't open, it's not your door.
Author Unknown

Whenever my grandchild would get upset or angry, we would tell her she needed to dispose of the anger or naughty words. She would take a walk to the bathroom, throw her anger into the toilet and flush it away. This small act would change her attitude immediately. She realized she had disposed of her misdeeds.

The thing we call "failure" is not the falling but the staying down.
Author Unknown

For as high as the heavens are above the earth, so great is his love for those who fear him; as far as the east is from the west, so far has he removed our transgressions from us.
Psalm 103:11-12 NIV

Give thanks to the Lord, for he is good; his love endures forever.
Psalm 107:1 NIV

A Miracle

Mike had purchased a used camping trailer and was tinkering around to see what needed to be fixed. He was inspecting all the systems to be sure they were working.

His daughter climbed the stairs to visit with her dad. After visiting for a while, she decided she was bored and went back outside.

Mike began working on the propane stove just as his daughter stepped outside. He lit a match and there was an instant explosion. His wife came running.

She realized immediately that he needed emergency care. In the emergency room, the doctor examined him, and determined that his burns were severe enough for him to be transported to a burn center. The doctor explained to Mike and his wife that he would need a lot of skin grafts to repair the second and third degree burns that had occurred during the blast. His face was badly burned, along with his arms and places on his torso. Against the advice of the emergency room doctor and his family, Mike went home that evening. He made a promise to seek medical help the next day from his family doctor.

After arriving home, his wife began calling church and family members and asking for prayers. There were numerous prayer chains praying for Mike.

When Mike and his wife awoke the next morning, they could not believe their eyes. The burns were practically non-existent. Mike and his wife met with the family doctor. When Mike explained the explosion and the severe burns, the doctor found it hard to believe that it had occurred. There were only signs of minor burns.

Prayers were answered. God healed Mike and saved him from the long ordeal of skin grafts due to his burns.

But let all who take refuge in you be glad; let them ever sing for joy. Spread your protection over them, that those who love your name may rejoice in you. For surely, O Lord, you bless the righteous; you surround them with your favor as with a shield.
Psalm 5:11-12 NIV

For God so loved the world that he gave his one and only Son, that whoever believes in him shall not perish but have eternal life.
John 3:16 NIV

God enters by a private door into every individual.

With God all things are possible.

Joyfulness keeps the heart and face young. A good laugh makes us better friends with ourselves and everybody around us.

Integrity

I carried a load of laundry to the basement to begin washing clothes for the day. I discovered the washer tub had fallen and was tilting to the side.

I phoned the business where I had purchased the washer and scheduled a repair time.

When the repairman arrived for the appointment, he checked the washer and said he would have to order the necessary parts for the repair.

When he returned with the parts a few days later, he informed me that the warranty would be expiring in three days. Because the washer was still under warranty, all the expenses for the repair were covered. Without the warranty we would have found it necessary to purchase a new washer due to the expense.

We were blessed because of the integrity and honesty of this man.

The next time you admire the wonderful things that God has made, remember that you're one of them.

"When I said, "My foot is slipping," your love, O Lord supported me. When anxiety was great within me, your consolation brought joy to my soul.
Psalm 94:18-19 NIV

Some of the closing words of the Bible are "Come, Lord Jesus." How many of us are denying ourselves of the love of our precious Lord and Savior by not inviting him into our lives.

For all have sinned and fallen short of the glory of God.
Romans 3:23 NIV

God is the same yesterday today and tomorrow.
Amen!

One Man….Two Boards….Three Nails
Redemption….Eternity

Faith Pulled Me Through

I am one of seven children. Growing up our parents taught us the value of respect, kindness and goodness. We attended church every Sunday.

Despite being honest, kind and intelligent, we were often overlooked for many things in life because of the mere fact that we were poor.

On the first day of first grade, I became friends with a girl named Stephanie. We are still friends to this day. She related to me that other girls wanted to be her friend. The other girl's parents would not allow them to play with her, if she continued to play with me. She chose me. I was blessed.

Being an outcast led me to seek a life of validation when I was young. For years I always wondered if I was good enough, pretty enough, had done enough. I needed approval and acceptance to feel good about myself. I had bought into the lie that I was not good enough. As I grew in faith, I discovered that I did not need validation. In God's eyes, I was all that I needed to be.

I praise you because I am fearfully and wonderfully made; your works are wonderful, I know that full well.
Psalm 139:14 NIV

Your beauty should not come from outward adornment, such as braided hair and the wearing of gold jewelry and fine clothes. Instead, it should be that of your inner self, the unfading beauty of a gentle and quiet spirit, which is of great worth in God's sight.
1 Peter 3:3-4 NIV

Travel Safety

We were traveling south from Indiana to our winter residence in Apache Junction, Arizona.

We had been fighting rain for several hundred miles and decided we should be tuned into the weather forecast. The weatherman was warning of an upcoming freezing rain.

After several phone calls, we discovered that all RV parks were closed in the area due to frozen water lines. We needed to get off the icy roads. We ended up in the parking lot of the Wal-Mart in Amarillo, Texas. By morning the parking lot was full of RVs. As the ice storm raged outside we were blessed to have heat via a generator. The generator was purchased just before we departed Indiana, it was the first and only time it was used. We had food, a bathroom and heat, all the comforts of home. We just had to ride out the icy storm.

I attempted an icy trek across the frozen parking lot to purchase a few necessities and an ice scraper. I was covered in safety, I slid but did not fall.

Once inside the store, I began searching for an ice scraper. I inquired of an employee where I might find one. He stated they were all sold out. He turned to walk away, then said "Wait! I just saw one in a cart that needs to be emptied." He ran and found the ice scraper and handed it to me.

After my return, Gordon stepped outside to assess the situation. The top step was frozen, his feet flew out from under him and he fell four feet to the pavement. He landed on his back, no injuries, no sore back, no bruises.

The roads from Amarillo, Texas to Albuquerque, New Mexico were closed. It was necessary to spend three days in the Wal-Mart parking lot.

After the storm subsided, Gordon had to place a ladder on the slippery pavement of the parking lot. It had been necessary to leave the largest slide-out open, as otherwise we would have had no seating. While standing on the ladder, he had to chip away at the ice accumulated on the canvas cover over the slide-out. Inch-by-inch he scraped as I held the door open and listened to instructions. I used the mechanism to move the slide-out in and out, very slowly. Gordon was protected from falling off the ladder and we were blessed that the slide-out was not destroyed by the heavy ice.

Before we left I offered the use of the ice scraper to others in the lot.

Preparations were complete, we were traveling to a fuel station. Gordon filled the tank with diesel fuel and then left the engine running while he went inside to pay. When he returned, he noticed blue smoke coming from the exhaust. At that moment, the engine died. Gordon went back inside to tell the attendant that the engine died after pumping diesel fuel. The attendant called the store manager.

The manager arrived and assessed the situation. There was water in the diesel fuel. All expenses would be paid by the company.

The truck was towed to a truck repair shop. Tanks and fuel lines were drained and blown out with air.
We waited there for hours for the repairs to be completed. After completion, we headed to Wal-Mart to pickup our 5th wheel and start heading south once again.

Gordon had to stop frequently as the engine sputtered and the exhaust continued to pour out blue smoke. The fuel filter needed drained periodically as there was still water in the fuel lines.

Forty miles outside of Tucumcari, New Mexico the engine stopped. Any attempt of starting the engine was futile. Diesel fuel was shooting out the side of the engine.

Gordon called the manager of the fuel station and advised him of our situation. He again said all expenses would be covered. He called for two tow trucks.

We were stranded on I-40 for five hours. Finally, two hot pink tow trucks arrived to rescue us. We rode in one tow truck while the other one hauled our 5th wheel to an RV park in Tucumcari. We spent three days in Tucumcari while the repairs were made.

We were blessed so many times on this trip. We were not aware when we parked in Wal-Mart that the highways would be closed for three days. We could have been stranded along the road with no heat. We would not have been able to use the generator along the highway. We could have had serious injuries due to the ice. We could have been stranded without an ice scraper and no way to close our slide-out. We were blessed many times over.

I can do anything through him who gives me strength. Philippians 4:13 NIV

I asked God, "Why are you taking me through troubled waters?" He replied, "Because your enemies can't swim."

We rented a car while we were in Tucumcari, New Mexico. Walking out of a local restaurant after breakfast, we climbed into the rental car. We noticed a man walking along the road carrying a fan belt. The temperature was approximately 20-25 degrees.

Gordon told me he felt he was being led to help this man. We turned around and Gordon called out to the man, offering him a ride. He stated his truck had broken down on the freeway. Gordon took him to the auto parts store a few blocks away and offered to take him back to his truck once he purchased the fan belt.

Traveling down the highway, he explained that he was carrying a load of wood from Texas to New Mexico. The weather was frigid, and his wife was concerned about him traveling so far in the freezing weather. She convinced him to take along a heavy coat and a blanket. He appreciated her wisdom. He was stranded and had spent the night in his truck. At first light he started walking. A truck driver had given him a ride several miles outside of town.

Gordon inquired if he knew Jesus. Yes, yes he said, I know Jesus. (He pronounced it in Spanish). He said his truck was approximately 5-10 miles away. It was 50 miles one-way. He was very close to the Texas border.

He called his wife and assured her he was fine. He explained to her that we might be strangers, but we were people like them, people who knew Jesus.

God protected this man from the elements. He had walked miles in sub-zero weather and slept in his vehicle in the freezing temperatures.

We were blessed to have been chosen to help this man during his time of trouble.

God is in the midst of our storms.

Everything you do is based on the choices you make. It's not your parents, your past relationships, your job, the economy, the weather, an argument or your age that is to blame. You and only you are responsible for every decision you make. When you have God in your life, those decisions, those mistakes and choices are lessened by His love.

So, we fix our eyes on not what is seen, but on what is unseen, since what is seen is temporary, but what is unseen is eternal.
2 Corinthians 4:18 NIV

But the fruit of the Spirit is love, joy, peace, forbearance, kindness, goodness, faithfulness, gentleness, and self-control. Against such things there is no law.
Galatians 5:22 NIV

As we ponder the great art of the Sistine Chapel by Michelangelo, the Mona Lisa by Leonardo Da Vinci and the School of Athens by Raphael, let us consider the art and beauty of my two-year-old granddaughter, as with crayons in hand, she colors the bathroom floor.

Consider the word "Time!" Pass time, in good time, mind the time, and be on time, out of time, etcetera. However, no matter how busy we are, we must always "Make time for God!"

If we don't teach our children to follow Christ, the world will teach them not to.

For it is with your heart that you believe and are justified, and it is with your mouth that you confess and are saved.
Romans 10:1 NIV

The Beatitudes

Blessed are the poor in spirit,
for theirs is the kingdom of heaven.
Blessed are those who mourn,
for they will be comforted.
Blessed are the meek,
for they shall inherit the earth.
Blessed are those who hunger and thirst for
righteousness,
for they will be filled.
Blessed are the merciful,
for they will be shown mercy.
Blessed are the poor in heart,
for they will see God.
Blessed are the peacemakers,
for they will be called sons of God.
Blessed are the those who are persecuted,
because of righteousness,
for theirs is the kingdom of heaven.
Matthew 5:3-10 NIV

Some of the Names of Jesus

King of Kings and Lord of Lords   Christ
Prophet   Master   Redeemer   I Am
Savior   Alpha and Omega
Immanuel   Nazarene   The Truth   Holy One
The Way   Lion of Judah   Messiah
Lamb of God   Shepherd   Friend
Son of God   Judge   God   Apostle
Word of God   Physician   Majesty
Counselor   Prince of Peace   Mediator

Be joyful always, pray continually, give thanks in all circumstances, for this is God's will for you in Jesus Christ.
1 Thessalonians 5:16-18 NIV

If you are God's child today, give thanks to Him for the inheritance held in trust for you in heaven - an inheritance that "does not fade away!"

I don't discriminate, I'm an equal opportunity hugger.

(F) orwarding
(A) ll
(I) ssues
(T) o
(H) eaven

Love makes our friends a little dearer
Joy makes our hearts a little lighter
Faith makes our paths a little clearer
Peace brings us all a little closer
Author Unknown

For the wages of sin is death, but the gift of God is eternal life in Christ Jesus our Lord.
Romans 6:23 NIV

But God demonstrates his own love for us in this: While we were still sinners, Christ died for us.
Romans 5:8 NIV

The Knot Prayer

Dear God,

Please untie the knots that are in my mind, my heart, and my life.

Remove the have nots, cannots, and the do nots.

Erase the will nots, may nots, might nots that may find a home in my heart.

Release me from the could nots, would nots, and should nots that obstruct my life.

And most of all, Dear God, I ask that you remove from my mind, my heart, and my life all of the "am nots" that I have allowed to hold me back. Especially the thought that I am not good enough. Amen
Author Unknown

He who has ears to hear, let him hear."
Luke 14:33 NIV

A Caring Lady

I was the co-pilot and controlled a 1928 Ford Tri-Motor airplane while flying over Goshen.

The 1928 Ford Tri-Motor airplane was the first all-air passenger service plane. It was inaugurated October 26, 1930.

My husband and I went to the Goshen Airport airshow on September 4, 2015 where he purchased a ticket for me to fly in this unique airplane.

Arriving ahead of the take-off time I had time to sit in the lobby of the airport. I met this wonderful woman who worked for the EAA – Experimental Aircraft Association. We had a wonderful time sharing our experiences and travels around the country.

She was scheduled to co-pilot that day but ended up gifting that opportunity to me. What an exciting experience. I will never forget her kindness!

Be thankful you don't already have everything you
desire,
If you did what would there be to look forward to?
Be thankful you don't know something
For it gives us an opportunity to learn.
Be thankful for each new challenge
Because it will build your strength and character.
Be thankful for your mistakes,
They will teach you valuable lessons.
Be thankful when you are tired and weary
Because it means you've made a difference.
It is easy to be thankful for the good things.
A life of rich fulfillment comes to those who are also
thankful for setbacks.
GRATITUDE can turn a negative into a positive.
Find a way to be thankful for your troubles and they can
become your blessings.
Author Unknown

Write your plans in pencil and give God the eraser!

In the morning when I rise give me Jesus.

My Mom

My mom was 5'2" and weighed 95 lbs. She was small in stature, but mighty in love and faith. I remember whenever she had to face struggles in life, she would say "I have faith to move mountains!"

My mom worked hard at raising seven children. I especially remember the summer months when she would can 800 quarts of fruits, vegetables, jams, jellies and juice and fill a chest type freezer. She took care of a large garden and her flower garden in the evenings.

I remember her getting up every morning to see my dad off to work at 5:30 A.M. He worked at Wright Patterson Air Force Base and had a 50-mile drive there and back each day. My dad arrived home around 5:30 every evening, my mom dutifully had dinner ready and waiting when he arrived.

Monday mornings she would set up the wringer washer to do laundry for nine people. Most days she would carry water in from the well to fill both the washer and rinse tub. I do remember my brothers pumping water from the well to fill the tubs the night before. Although the tubs were prefilled, there was still water that needed to be brought in and heated in the kitchen. The water would then have to be carried to the back porch to place in the tubs. This was a Monday morning task that took place during summer months, during snowy days or during the rain. My mom did this task without complaint. It took nearly all day for mom to finish the laundry. My sisters and I helped in the summer months. The laundry always smelled so clean and refreshing after hanging in the fresh air.

Mom taught us values of love, sharing, honesty, good manners and brought us up in faith. She read us the Uncle Remus series of *Brier Fox and Brier Bear*, along with the Bible daily. We asked for one more story, one more chapter, but she would say we had to wait till the next evening. She would gently place these books in her linen drawer until the next evening. An amazing part of this story is that my mom, due to health issues, only had a third-grade education.

This small woman had a giant-sized heart. She is now walking with the angels. Love you mom.

From the rising of the sun to the place where it sets, the name of the Lord is to be praised. The Lord is exalted over all the nations, his glory above the heavens. Who is like the Lord our God, the One who sits enthroned on high, who stoops down to look on the heavens and the earth?
Psalm 113:3-6 NIV

Then he said to them all: "If anyone would come after me, he must deny himself and take up his cross daily and follow me."
Luke 9:23 NIV

Only two defining forces have died for you - Jesus Christ and the American soldier. One died for your sins, the other died for your freedom. We honor, salute and thank you – the past and present men and women who have served our country. God Bless America!

Don't put people down, instead put them on your prayer list.

We have different gifts, according to the grace given us. If a man's gift is prophesying, let him use it in proportion to his faith. If it is serving, let him serve; if it is teaching, let him teach; if it is encouraging, let him encourage; if it is contributing to the needs of others, let him give generously; if it is leadership, let him govern diligently; if it is showing mercy, let him do it cheerfully.
Romans 12:6-8 NIV

We use different methods to help our granddaughter, Addison, with her spelling words. We rhyme, we sing, we break down words within words. We have started the process of teaching her the Books of the Bible. We have begun with the first five books. So, she says, "Genesis, Exodus, struggles with the pronunciation of Leviticus, says Numbers and "letters" (staring with those mischievous big blue eyes and smiles) and struggles with Deuteronomy. I encourage with Deu and she says, "Do it right." We will work on that one. She is making progress.

Cast all your anxiety on God because he cares for you.
1 Peter 5:7 NIV

When we invite Jesus into every aspect of our lives, he can exchange our past pain for present comfort and turn our sorrow into divine delight. He can take old wounds and turn them into fresh wisdom. If we just ask, he can take those things that we are ashamed of and cast them into a sea of forgetfulness, allowing us to experience truth and deep joy. He does not save the best for last, he saves the best for now.

Yet for us, there is but one God, the Father, from whom all things came and for whom we live; and there is but one Lord, Jesus Christ, and through him who all things came and through whom we live.
1 Corinthians 8:6 NIV

Parenting ABC's

A-lways trust your children to God's care.

B-ring them to church.

C-hallenge them to high goals.

D-elight in their achievements.

E-xalt the Lord in their presence.

F-rown on evil.

G-ive them love.

H-ear their problems.

I-gnore not their childish fears.

J-oyfully accept their apologies.

K-eep their confidence.

L-ive a good example before them.

M-odel by example those qualities you want your child to have.

N-ever ignore their endless questions.

O-pen your heart to their love.

P-ray for them by name.

Q-uicken your interest in their spirituality.

R-emember their needs.

S-how them the way of salvation.

T-each them to work.

U-nderstand they are still young.

V-erify your statements.
W-eather trials together as a family.
eX-pect changes to occur in the family
Y-earn for God's best for them.
Z-ealously guide them in Bible truth.
Author Unknown

The Lord is my light and my salvation – whom shall I fear? The Lord is the stronghold of my life – of whom shall I be afraid?
Psalm 27:1 NIV

My husband and I were sitting on the deck and enjoying the sunshine. There was not a cloud in the sky. Then I chanced to look up at the sky again. The only cloud in the sky was a large handprint. This was surely a sign from God. His presence was surrounding our community.

Loved you yesterday
Love you still
Always have
Always will

A Kind Heart

Preparing to go into junior high for a shy girl was a transition within itself without having to face "The Bear." Previous students led everyone to believe that the teacher was very strict and a no-nonsense teacher. The teacher was over 6' tall, a plus size man, wore a crew cut, and had a booming voice. Everyone was warned pre-junior high about how rigid he was in the classroom. He was nicknamed "The Bear."

This "big man" had a gentle heart. Oh yes, if truth be known, I'm sure he would have liked perfection. I saw a gentler side of him. He loved to tell stories and funny witticisms.

One day he changed my life for me, and I will always remember his kindness. He was filling out report cards, then stopped momentarily. He began a conversation stating that he normally does not point out students, but there was someone he felt needed to be recognized. He then called my name and asked me what grade I was receiving in each subject. I responded with either an A or B with each subject. He confirmed in front of the class that I was correct. When he asked about the math grade, I shyly hesitated and then said, "You're the math teacher, and I think you know the answer to that question." He laughed. He said he wanted the other students to know that I was a good student.

He told the students that our circumstances do not take away the intelligence we have and display. This moment changed my life. He informed the other students that money, prestige or looks are not what define us. We should view people, as a complete person, rather than a part.

He said it was time I was given the attention I deserved. He MADE A DIFFERENCE IN MY LIFE. He instilled confidence in me. This small act encouraged me to face life with a positive attitude. It made me aware that there were people outside of my immediate family that cared. I applied myself and maintained an honor roll status throughout high school. One small act from a caring teacher made a difference.

I'm praying for blessings for teachers everywhere!

A Letter from Kozmo

Kimi, I thought you might like to hear of my "pup" adventures with mom and dad. They are not my "Dog"ological parents, but rather my "people" parents. We have traveled over 3,500 miles (many puppy steps.)

We traveled 805 miles the first day. I did not think "dad" would ever stop. I had a comfortable bed in the back seat, but I was "dog-tired."

"Dad" took us to see his home town where he was raised. We visited his childhood school that was a one-room school. It has been converted to a three-room school now. This was nothing like my "obedience school." I was outside when I received my education.

We visited the post office where "dad's" mom was a postmistress (I guess that is like a woman boss at the post office.) "Dad" talked about his childhood and teen years.

We crossed the Golden Gate Bridge in San Francisco, California. WOW! That would be one big bath if you fell into that body of water.

We visited a place called Alcatraz. It is a prison where they used to keep bad "dawgs." I'm a good pup, I would not have to stay there. "Mom" and "dad" were just visitors. Whew, I would not like leaving them there!

We then traveled to the Redwood Forest in Eureka, California. I was amazed at the size of the redwood trees. "Mom" and "dad" were walking around and taking pictures. "Mom" looked up and saw my big brown eyes staring at her, I was begging to get out and run around all those trees. "Mom" said it was too muddy for me. "Aw C'mon, I could get another bath!"

"Dad" was standing by the "biggedest" tree I have ever seen. "Pup O' Pup!" How I wanted to get out and lift my leg there. "Dad" said the tree was 2,400 years old. Hmm! In puppy years that would be 16,100 years. We saw a lot of those trees, but I did not get to utilize even one of them. Oh, puppy tails and toenails.

We stayed in a motel and I was very good. I crawled into bed with "Mom". She said "dad" and I both snored and I needed some puppy toothpaste and mouthwash!

Puppy "Breath" Kisses and Paw Prints to you.

Love,

Kozmo

We rescued Kozmo from a shelter. He traveled across the US and Canada with us. We soon discovered he could speak, roll over, shake his paw, fetch, and jump hurdles. The kids loved him.

For every animal of the forest is mine, and the cattle on a thousand hills. I know every bird in the mountains, and the insects in the fields are mine.
Psalm 50:10-11

Childhood Memories

I am thankful for childhood memories. We were a family of seven children. We sat around the kitchen table every night for dinner and everyone took their turn saying a prayer at each meal.

In the summer months we were our own baseball team. One of my brothers was the pitcher and everyone knew I was an easy out. I couldn't recall how many windows were broken.

We played Red Rover, Goosey Goosey Gander, baseball and Tag You're It. After dark, we played Hide and Seek or Tag You're It, while running and hiding within a block in any direction. It was the "good old days" when we were not fearful, we did not have to worry about our safety. We would stay out till dark, or until mom or dad would call us inside.

We would sit out on evenings and watch the stars or see who could catch the most fireflies.

I remember fun times with my sister, Patti. We built tents by placing blankets over the clotheslines. Occasionally, we would make two tents, so we could visit one another. We would play with dolls, dishes, read and play school.

Patti and I were given a pair of roller skates that we were supposed to share. We liked it when we could use both skates, but sometimes we would both use one skate. Around and around the block we would skate. I remember Patti asking for her turn with both skates. I'd remark "Just another time around the block (or two)." I was selfish sometimes, sorry Patti. If I could skate now, I would be more kind and buy two pairs of skates and invite Patti to the roller rink.

Inside games that we played consisted of jacks, dominoes, Monopoly, Battleship, tic tac toe, checkers and chess. We did not have an electronic game, we drew our own graphs to play Battleship.

My dad used his pocketknife and let everyone take a turn at hiding it. Everyone came up with clever locations to hide the knife. When it was my turn, I might as well have stood in the middle of the floor and held the knife. Everyone hid the knife well, me – not so much. One evening, when my turn came around, and with every eye closed, my dad let me hide the knife in his shirt pocket. There was victory that night. No one could figure out the location of the hidden pocketknife. The clues – you are getting warmer, warmer, you are hot, still did not reveal the location of the pocketknife. Everyone finally gave up and I was victorious. Thanks for the memory dad.

We went to church every Sunday. Dad usually did the cooking on Sundays. His favorite meal was meatloaf, prepared in the pressure cooker. Yum!

I was involved with the youth ministry at church, sang in the youth choir, and was a Sunday school secretary. Twice while singing in church I was caught up in the music and continued singing the next verse when everyone else had stopped. One Sunday, the pastor was singing "How Great Thou Art." Everyone was joining in with the chorus. I knew every word to that song, I just kept on singing when everyone else stopped. The pastor stopped and invited me to sing along with him. I declined. My one chance to sing and I declined. My talents lie elsewhere.

I remember mom's beautiful flower garden. I loved the smell of the lilacs and hyacinths, and the beauty of the lilies, roses and gladiolus. Mom loved her flowers, she had a large garden approximately 20' x 30', also flowers blooming all around the house. She tended her garden with loving care.

Mom had two bushes with tiny pink flowers, Patti and I used to make headbands with them every summer.

Mom also tended her grape vines. When the grapes were ripe, my sisters and I would help her make grape jelly and juice. I have wonderful memories of a large vat of water simmering until it turned purple. The aroma was overwhelming. The grapes were then put through a grinder to turn them into pulp, the pulp was then put through a sieve until it was clear and ready to be made into juice or jelly. Fond memories!

We lived a couple of blocks from the elementary school and played there often. I remember my dad's whistle (cupping your hands together and blowing.) When you heard this whistle, it was time to have your skirt tails and shirt tails flying. There were no second chances, no tardiness. My brothers and I learned to whistle in this manner, cannot recall my sisters ever learning.

My parents raised us with little money, but what they had, they shared, and what we didn't have we did without. We did have lots of love. We felt safe at night, and we were happy, so I guess we had all we needed and then some.

Train up a child in the way he should go, and when he is old he will not turn from it.
Proverbs 22:6 NIV

As for me and my household, we will serve the Lord.
Joshua 24:15 NIV

Sons are a heritage from the Lord, children a reward
from him.
Psalm 127:3 NIV

Happiness keeps you sweet
Trials keep you strong
Failures keep you humble
Success keeps you glowing
God keeps you going
Author Unknown

Be kind, for everyone you meet is fighting a battle you
know nothing about.

I am so thankful to have an attitude of gratitude.

Happiness cannot be traveled to, owned, earned, worn
or consumed. Happiness is the spiritual experience of
living every minute with love, grace, and gratitude.

If only we have the will to walk, then God is pleased with our stumbles.

For I know the plans I have for you, declares the Lord, plans to prosper you and not to harm you, plans to give you hope and a future.
Jeremiah *29:11 NIV*

It doesn't matter where you go in life or what you do – It's who you have beside you.

Life has taught us that love does not consist in gazing in at each other, but in looking outward together in the same direction.
Author Unknown

Everyone smiles in the same language.

Joy of Grandchildren

My oldest grandson, Dylan, was primarily exposed to adults in his formative years. His intelligence and vocabulary were well beyond his age. He could amaze you with his stories and insight.

The one story I remember the most and still makes me laugh, was regarding a moth. Papa was carrying Dylan down the street, and I was walking beside them. He was still attached to a pacifier at this age. He had the habit of spitting out the pacifier if he saw someone with food.

This day, he spit out his pacifier and I looked around for someone with food. However, he surprised his papa and me and said, "Hurry up papa, hurry up. Moths eat old things and you are old. You must get inside." We both laughed so hard. No idea the origin of this story.

Later in the day, we were at his great-grandmother's house. I relayed the moth story to her and she laughed. Dylan said, "Why are you laughing, you are old too, the moth could eat you too.

Letter to the Coach

My daughter had been told repeatedly to clean her room. It was cluttered with dirty clothes, dirty dishes, candy wrappers, pop cans, etc.

I warned her if she did not get the room cleaned, all privileges would be taken from her. She would not be allowed outside of her room, other than school, until it was cleaned.

One morning, I told her to be home immediately after school to clean her room. "But mom, I have track practice, I cannot miss. The coach will be upset and not let me run in the track meet." "I'm sorry, you have been warned. I'll write an excuse for the teacher."

The excuse was something like this:

Coach _____,

I am sorry that my daughter was not present for track practice yesterday. You see, I love my daughter very much. The circumstances of her missing practice are somewhat like this explanation:

I have repeatedly asked her to clean her room and she has failed to complete this task. I warned her that non-compliance of this request would create a negative outcome for her.

Her bedroom looks like a war zone. Why she would ever dare to step inside that myriad of a mess is beyond me! I have been worried as to the height of the debris in her room. I'm concerned if she begins digging her way through the mess, she may keep digging and digging until she reaches China. My thinking is if she starts now, maybe she has a chance, perhaps she will only dig a hole into the basement.

She finally realized I was serious and has cleaned said room. She did not dig as far as the basement, as I anticipated. Hopefully, she will keep her room clean and will not miss anymore track practices.

After this excuse, I don't remember any of my children requiring one. Humor can be the best medicine.

****

My Children

My four children have been sources of joy, love and laughter. As the saying goes, never a dull moment. Their day-to-day escapades were enough to make you laugh yourself silly or be stress-filled depending on both their moods and mine. I was blessed with four beautiful, happy children. One was born a day after my husband's and my anniversary, one the day after his dad's birthday, one on Christmas Day, and one two days before Thanksgiving. It made for some interesting holidays.

Our family activities included backyard games of badminton, baseball and snowball fights. The joy and happiness of those times are caught in photos and movies.

The kitchen was always a buzz of activity. I love to cook and bake. Baking was generally a weekly event in our household with me baking triple or quadruple batches of cookies. Nearly every time I baked or made fudge, the house would be filled with my children's friends. But, for the life of me, I could not figure out how they knew I was baking or making fudge. When I would inquire, some of the neighborhood kids would just say, "We could smell them all the way down the street!" Okay! I guess I didn't really buy into that, but I was willing to share. It was not until years later when my group explained, "When you lit the oven, we started with the phone calls."

Mom's baking times included making 144 dozen cookies with a friend. We passed them out for holiday gift giving. The children were always present to be the "taste testers!"

Accidents happen in life, but we were spared limited ones with our children. My memories include my son taking the cover off the floor vent and tying to climb through. He started falling and landed in a bar stool in the basement. He scraped his arms and sides, but it was minimal compared to what could have happened. One of my daughters was somersaulting across the kitchen floor, when her brother decided to open the basement door. She somersaulted down the stairs and landed on the basement floor. No injuries, just hurt pride and anger at her brother. My second son, was reaching for something in the utensil drawer and because someone had not sheathed a sharp knife, he needed stitches. I was grateful for neighbors that evening, too much red for me. The youngest daughter was seated in my lap and continued to bounce forward. I was putting my hand in front of her to stop her from hitting her head. I was distracted once and sure enough, she hit the table and ended up in the emergency room.

We had a neighbor who kept us supplied with eggs and fruits and vegetables. I remember making batches of orange marmalade one summer, and canning vegetables thanks to her kindness.

Sunday evenings were designated as family night. We watched Family Classics, Disney movies, WGN and sat in front of the TV set for dinner. Sunday dinner was always cake and ice cream.

Saturday mornings were cartoon days. We had the children on a rotating schedule so that everyone had a chance to watch their favorite cartoons.

Backyard BBQ's were a favorite. There were even winter days when dad would bundle up and light the BBQ fire. Hot dogs and hamburgers were the favorites. There were some great meals based on those BBQ's. Memorable BBQ's were having 40-60 people over during 4th of July celebrations and watching the fireworks afterwards.

We traveled to Ohio nearly every summer to visit family and friends. There are stories of riding on a four-wheeler and climbing the hills "down on the farm." There was camping and campfires. There were spooky stories told in the dark.

When the children were pre-school age, I would watch educational TV shows with them and count, sing-a-long or share the show's activities with the little ones.

The children remember the weekend trips to Michigan to visit their grandmother. According to them she had the same meal every time, "Shake 'n Bake" Chicken, Parker house rolls and mashed potatoes and gravy. They remember grandma laughing at their silly antics.

The children remember me reading to them frequently. I would change my voices for the different characters in the book. My favorite was the "Cookie Monster" book and those voice change-overs.

My son, keep your father's command and do not forsake your mother's teaching.
Proverbs 6:20 NIV

God blessed us with beautiful, caring children. I cherish the memories. My family is my greatest treasure.

About the Author

Mary Foster is a wife, mother of four children, grandmother of 9 children and a great-grandmother of 2 children. She loves to craft, currently involved in making 3-D greeting cards that she uses for a ministry. She loves to cook and bake and shares recipes and food with family and neighbors. She is excited about her book, something that has been on her "Bucket List" for a long time. She is praying that readers will be blessed by this book and will share it with others.

ACKNOWLEDGMENTS

Gordon, on good days and difficult days during this journey, you have been my main support. Thanks for understanding when I made toast for dinner. Thanks for helping me edit and giving me breaks. The few pages you typed from my scribbles helped. Thanks for the times I looked cross-eyed and you continued to pass out encouragement, faith in my abilities and lots of love and hugs. This book would not have made it to press without you.

Linda, you have blessed me by offering to teach a writing class. I'm not sure I would have fulfilled this item on my "Bucket List" without your encouragement. Thanks for all the computer help. They say you "can't teach old dogs new tricks," but I think we have proved that theory wrong. You'll never know how much your kindness and patience are appreciated.

Shari, the first rough draft of my fledgling pages, were proofed by you. Thanks for the support and confidence. It gave this "senior" the ability to push through the editing and re-editing that she found necessary. I appreciate the prayers and friendship.

Stephanie, WOW, where has the time flown? Was it really 60+ years ago - the day we met on the first day of 1st grade. Maintaining a friendship all these years is special. Retirement looks good on you. Thanks so much for reading my final draft through the eyes of a retired school teacher. Our friendship so many years ago set the stage for bigger and brighter futures. Thanks so much for hanging in there.

88859655R00053

Made in the USA
Lexington, KY
18 May 2018